Oats!

Happy Holidays
Suzanne & John +
John H.

love Mama

The motto I proposed...was: Tenui musam medi tamur avena —
"We cultivate literature upon a little oatmeal."

—Rev. Sydney Smith, Works 1859

Oats!

A Book of Whimsy

by Shirley Streshinsky
& Maria Streshinsky

Celestial Arts
Berkeley, California

Many of the designations used by manufacturers and sellers to distinguish their products are claimed as trademarks. Where the publisher is aware of a trademark claim, such designations, in this book, have initial capital letters.

Celestial Arts
P.O. Box 7123
Berkeley, California 94707

A Kirsty Melville Book

Distributed in Australia by E.J. Dwyer Pty. Ltd., in Canada by Publishers Group West, in New Zealand by Tandem Press, in South Africa by Real Books, in the United Kingdom and Europe by Airlift Books, and in Singapore and Malaysia by Berkeley Books.

Cover and interior design by Nancy Austin

Library of Congress Cataloging-in-Publication Data
   Streshinsky, Shirley.
      Oats! : a book of whimsy / by Shirley Streshinsky & Maria Streshinsky.
            p.   cm.
      ISBN 0-89087-808-0 (pbk.)
      1. Cookery (Oats)   2. Oats.   I. Streshinsky, Maria, 1969-   II. Title.
   TX809.O23S77   1996
   641.6'313--DC20   96-28778
                                                            CIP

First printing, 1996
Printed in Canada

1 2 3 4 5 6 - 00 99 98 97 96

If your mama ever told you to eat your oats,
you'll want this book.

Hello???? The mighty Food and Drug Administration has finally caught on to what our mamas knew all along. In January of 1996, after reviewing the results of 30 years of research and 41 clinical trials, the FDA proposed the first food-specific health claim—for oatmeal, of course:

- *Diets high in oatmeal and low in saturated fat and cholesterol may reduce the risk of heart disease.*

As we go to press, the FDA is preparing its final ruling. Keep your eye on the news for an update…

Contents

All boys need to sow some wild oats.

—Rose Kennedy **must** *have said this*

During icy-cold January weeks, Americans spend
about $6 million on oatmeal.

Introduction

Oats, often in the form of oatmeal, have been a mainstay in the lives of many of us—as nourishment, as comfort, and as something harder to define. Oats echo in the memories of those of us who grew up in cold climes. Our mothers knew that this most unpretentious of grains, offered up steaming hot on a cold winter morning, had powers beyond nutrition. They told us, so often and with such unshakable faith that it became deeply embedded in our psyches, that oatmeal would stick to our ribs, it would watch over us and comfort us, make us brave and healthy and wise. In the pursuit of happiness, oatmeal would sustain. In a world prone to chaos, it would encourage order. We learned that if we eat our oats, we will be properly fueled for whatever inclement weather, either meteorological or emotional, lies ahead. We understand now that even as the simple, lowly oat works its wonders on the digestive tract, doing battle with cholesterol and vanquishing the likes of the ghastly diverticulitis, it is working its transcendental wonders on the psyche.

You scoff.

Read on.

Basically, here's what you need to know to join the oat cognoscenti:

Say this aloud: Its inflorescence is a graceful, spreading panicle.

Translation: The oat stem blossoms into a graceful, spreading cluster of flowers.

Now you are proficient in oatspeak.

Oatmeal is made by removing the outer husk of the oat kernel. The groat, or inner portion of the kernel, contains the thin layers of bran (which can be removed to form oat bran) and the oat germ. When the groats are cut into pieces, the result is "steel cut" oats. (The Brits call them "pinhead.") When these pieces are softened by steam (in the process they are partially cooked) and flattened on rollers to form flakes, they become "rolled oats." The finer the flakes, the faster the rolled oat can be cooked, thus five minute, three minute, and instant oats.

Oat aficionados prefer steel cut. These can be purchased in sophisticated little packets or imported tins in expensive shops, or they can be bought in bulk at health food stores for not much more than the rolled variety.

Once upon a time, this hardy steel cut variety was food for the poor. Now it is the choice of the intelligentsia.

———

A short and decidedly inconclusive history of oats

Oats: Cereal plants of the genus *Avena* of the family *Gramineae* (grass family). The early history of oats is obscure, but domestication is considered to be recent compared to that of the other grains—perhaps c. 2500 B.C. During the Bronze Age, the time when horses were first used as draft animals, oats were widely grown in Northern Europe but were apparently still uncultivated by the civilizations around the Mediterranean.

—*Columbia Encyclopedia*, 5th edition 1993

A cereal, probably native to the Mediterranean basin, and cultivated in temperate regions.

—*The Cambridge Encyclopedia*, Cambridge University Press

———

Oats were one of the earliest cereals cultivated by man. They were known in ancient China as long ago as 7000 B.C. while the Greeks are the first people known to have made a recognizable porridge from oats. It was the Romans who not only introduced oats to other countries in Europe, but also gave them and other cultivated grasses the name cereals, after Ceres, the Roman goddess of agriculture.

In the U.K., Scotland, the north of England, and Northern Ireland had the most suitable climate for growing oats and by the Sixth century oats were established in Scotland alongside barley as a popular cereal crop. The Romans called the cereal they had introduced "good for the savages of Northern Europe."

—*The Oat Cookbook*, Mary Cadogan and Shirley Bond

In 1854, an immigrant miller named Ferdinand Schumacher set up a small mill in Ohio to turn out oats for oatmeal, in the belief that it was a superbly nourishing and cheap human food. At first, only the German, Scottish, and Irish immigrants believed him; at the time, the American breakfast table groaned under a weight of rabbit, squirrel, salt fish, venison, sausages, ham and bacon, potatoes and vegetables, pies and buckwheat cake, and on and on. Irish and German immigrants poured into the country in the 1870s and 80s, and they all bought oatmeal from the single source. Thirty years later, Schumacher had made a fortune and was known as The Oatmeal King. He had convinced Americans that oatmeal was healthy for them, and his Rolled Avena became popular up and down the Eastern Seaboard, as far west as Denver, and was even being exported to Scotland, that sanctuary for oats. Schumacher's innovative milling techniques set the stage for the growth of the Quaker Oats Company.

A *New York Times* editorial joked, "Of course [a Scotchman] does not like [oatmeal] any more than he likes his hereditary Calvinism, but he is entirely willing to eat it as long as it is cheap…If the oatmeal craze continues, the next generation of Americans will be as dyspeptic and Calvinistic as the majority of Scotchmen." People began to think of oatmeal as a nutritious and cheap food.

By the 1880s, Henry Parsons Crowell of Ravenna, Ohio, was selling his rolled oats under the brand name Quaker. More than one hundred years and many ground-breaking merchandising innovations later, Quaker Oats is still the biggest-selling hot breakfast cereal in the world. Today, eighty percent of all U.S. households have oatmeal in their pantries, two-thirds of it in the familiar round package with the Quaker Oats man smiling out. Quaker's oats are sold in 25 countries around the world. The average American eats 15 bowls of oatmeal a year; altogether, Americans spend a whopping $650 million for the pleasure.

> *His product was good and his methods unusual: he put up two-pound measures of his oatmeal in filthproof paper boxes, with explicit cooking directions on the carton.*
>
> *—From Brands, Trademarks, and Good Will, the Story of the Quaker Oats Company by Arthur F. Marquette*

A GLOSSARY OF OAT TERMINOLOGY

groats....oats after the hull is removed

rolled oats....groats that have been steamed and flattened on rollers

steel cut oats.....groats that are cut but not rolled

porridge..........oatmeal, almost always

mush................oatmeal, most of the time

Food for Your Heart: Oats and Health

You have to eat oatmeal or you'll dry up. Anybody knows that.

—Eloise, in Kay Thompson's *Eloise*

A BRIEF NUTRITIONAL PROFILE:

One cup of oatmeal (that's 1/2 cup dry oats) contains 150 calories, 27 grams carbohydrate, 5 grams protein, 4 grams dietary fiber (both soluble and insoluble), and only 3 grams of naturally occurring fat.

Translation: In addition to being high in fiber and low in fat, oats are cholesterol-free, sodium-free, and a good source of complex carbohydrates. They also contain more protein than any other major grain.

When most people think about the effect of oats on health, they remember the oat bran craze of the late 1980s, when oatmeal was touted as the silver bullet in lowering cholesterol. Sales of Quaker Oat Bran soared—from 1 million pounds in 1987 to more than 20 million pounds just two years later. Some 300 new oat-bran products were rushed to market; suddenly, everybody was putting oat bran into everything, even potato chips. It was a health craze that seized the nation. Robert E. Kowalski's *8-week*

Cholesterol Cure (or "How I Saved My Life by Eating Three Oatbran Muffins a Day") generated sales of $40 million.

Although 30 years of research pointed to the benefits of oats when consumed as part of a low-fat diet, a contradictory study soon popped up to dispute oats' cholesterol-lowering power. This study received national media attention as well, and soon the American public was off in search of the next magical food. But the question remained: Can oats improve cardiovascular health? In the intervening years, scientists continued to study the potential benefits of oats, and Congress passed a major food labeling law, setting up a specific process for food producers to make health claims for their products. Now, based on the scientific evidence, the FDA has thrown its hat into the ring on the side of the yea-sayers by proposing the first food-specific claim for oatmeal.

But just how much oatmeal does one need to eat every day to reap the health benefits, and how does it work? Studies show that a large bowl—around 1 1/2 cups of cooked oatmeal made from 3/4 cup rolled oats—will achieve the desired cholesterol-lowering benefits. The soluble fiber in oats contains beta-glucan, which forms a gel in the small intestine during digestion. The gel surrounds cholesterol-rich bile acids and prevents them from being reabsorbed into the bloodstream. As a result, the liver pulls more cholesterol out of the bloodstream to make a new supply of bile acids, and cholesterol levels drop.

Although cardiovascular benefits may be the most widely known reason to eat more oats, some studies show that the soluble fiber in oats may have other positive health effects as well. For example, it's believed that the high rates of such ailments as cancer and diabetes in industrialized countries today result as much from low intake of fiber-rich grains, fruits, and vegetables as from over consumption of high-fat animal foods. Oats can play a big part in increasing fiber intake to a more healthful level. For those already suffering from diabetes, oats can help prevent the sharp insulin spikes that occur with many other foods.

The fiber in oats can also be a powerful antidote to painful digestive disorders caused in part by lack of fiber in the diet. For example, when white bread and flour became all the rage, a nation of possible sufferers of diverticulitis was born. The condition arises from the inflammation of the colon's mucous membrane, which causes pockets to form in the large intestine. Waste matter gets trapped and can cause infection and inflammation—but one way to hold the disease at bay is to eat plenty of fiber, such as oat bran. Colitis, an inflammation of the mucous membrane of the colon, is another nasty customer that can be treated with bran. A concoction of oat bran and steamed or raw vegetables mixed in the blender is recommended to help cleanse the colon. Another remedy: one tablespoon of oat or rice bran daily, added to cereals or juice.

- *Some research shows that oatmeal can even make dieting easier because it keeps you feeling full longer.*

- *If faulty digestion gives you halitosis (the nice name for bad breath), try adding a tablespoon of oat bran to a glass of juice twice a day.*

When my mother learned she had developed adult-onset diabetes and had to change her diet drastically, I wondered how she could possibly give up the beloved scrambled eggs mixed with fried salami or lox, her eggs and onions, or the bakery fresh rye and challah she slathered with whipped butter. How could she—a Jewish mother to the core—survive on the carefully measured portions of dry toast and plain, ungarnished oatmeal recommended by the AMA for breakfast?

At first I felt guilty when she took out her plain box of oatmeal with the special measuring cup she kept buried inside, poured her cereal into boiling water and stirred it, then prepared my eggs and toast while it was cooking. Soon, though, something miraculous happened—she embraced her new diet with passion. In very little time, I could see that my mother actually began looking forward to her daily cereal. The oatmeal comforted her.

In time, that bowl of sustenance came to symbolize my mother. Instead of dwelling on the diet's restrictions and limitations, she relished her new foods with gusto and grace. This is how she took care of herself; it is also how she defined her style.

Until recently, I could never fathom eating oatmeal. Now I am about the same age as my mother was when she began her breakfast ritual, and I find that, topped with nonfat milk and honey or brown sugar, oats are satisfying any time of the day.

—Karen Dash is a writer and mother
living in Berkeley, California

Oats aren't just good for your insides—they're also an inexpensive and easy way to soothe and pamper your skin.

According to the UC Berkeley Wellness Letter's November 1995 issue, oats can provide relief from sunburn and reduce inflammation. Just scatter a cup into a tub of cool water and take a soak, or try wrapping uncooked oats in cheesecloth and dropping the pouch in the bath water. The Wellness Letter also recommends colloidal oatmeal (sold in drugstores) as a poison ivy remedy.

But that's not all. The Nutra Soothe Colloidal Oatmeal Bath package lists many other reasons to use their oat-based product: it provides soothing temporary relief of itching due to dry skin, chicken pox, rashes, eczema, psoriasis, poison ivy, poison oak, poison sumac, insect bites, hives, sunburn, prickly heat. Helps treat and prevent diaper rash. Protects minor skin irritations due to diaper rash.

Or perhaps you're just looking for a spa experience? Oats can play a part here too, as part of a relaxing bath or beauty masque you can make in just a few minutes.

Oatmeal, Rice, and Coconut Bath

To soften, smooth, and rehydrate rough, dry, tired skin.

1 cup rolled oats, quick or old-fashioned

1 cup uncooked brown rice

1 teaspoon coconut extract

*5 black tea bags (emptied) or 2 tablespoons
   loose tea*

Mix all ingredients in a mixing bowl. Divide mixture in half, storing one half in a covered container for future use. Place the other half of the mixture into an 8-inch by 8-inch cheesecloth square; tie into a pouch with a string. Run a bath with very hot water and submerge the pouch in the water. Squeeze the pouch a few times to fully hydrate the ingredients. When water has cooled to a comfortable temperature, slip into bath. Pouch may remain in bath. Try to stay in the water for at least 30 minutes for full benefit.

Makes enough for 2 baths

Recipe courtesy of Philip B., from his book *Blended Beauty*
(Ten Speed Press, 1995)

A Hawaiian Oatmeal-Papaya Beauty Masque

Created by Connie Gayle for her beauty center in the Kahala Mandarin Oriental Hotel in Honolulu.

FOR NORMAL SKIN

1/2 cup cooked oatmeal

1 whole egg

1 tablespoon kukui oil (available at beauty supply and natural foods stores)

1/2 cup mashed papaya

FOR OILY SKIN

1/2 cup cooked oatmeal

1 egg white

1 tablespoon fresh lemon juice

1/2 cup mashed apple

1 tablespoon kaolin

1 tablespoon bentonite

FOR DRY SKIN

1/2 cup cooked oatmeal

1 egg yolk

1/2 banana, mashed

1 tablespoon kukui oil

1/2 cup mashed papaya

Mix ingredients into a smooth paste. Spread on face and leave for 15 minutes. Rinse with tepid water and pat dry.

HEALTH LORE

- *According to Russian folklore, pneumonia can be dispatched with a poultice of equal parts hot oatmeal and hot dry mustard.*

- *Oatmeal topped with fried onions? The Germans tout it as a cure for a hangover.*

- *In the Swiss Alps, frostbite is sometimes treated with a paste of oats.*

We don't eat the stuff, we put it on our faces.

—Kimberly Parsons, a pretty Texas lady

Reveries and Memories

I know why my mother wanted to write this book. She has this affection—well, really it's an obsession—for oats. Probably she's had it since she left the winter-frozen Midwest for the mild, temperate west coast. It's as if oats are an unfaltering tie to growing up, oats are childhood, oats are a coat of armor in the biting cold and against the storms of life, oats are an homage to a loving mother.

Mom didn't let the fact that my brothers and I were west-coast-grown stop her from insisting on our shoveling in the oats the minute the thermometer dropped below sixty degrees. On those mornings, we'd stagger down the hall, groggy with sleep, and she'd be there smiling (part of her problem is an ultramorningperson personality), and she'd say, "You need your oatmeal," in very much the way another mother might tell a diabetic child, "You need your insulin." We resorted to heroic measures to avoid the sticky mush. We begged for pancakes, French toast, even eggs on occasion, but it was no use. Mom was hell-bent on transferring her faith in oats to her offspring.

Years later, I found myself in Utah when snow was falling, the temperature plunging. I stepped into the hotel restaurant for breakfast, sat down, and before the waiter could bring me a menu, blurted out exactly what I knew I needed: "Just a bowl of oatmeal please."

My next thought was: "Sweet Jesus, I've been converted."

—Maria Streshinsky

When I was a child, every morning I was given cod liver oil, which I hated, hot cereal, which I loved, with butter melting on top, and a pitcher of heavy cream. That was good mothering.

—Barbara Kafka, *Microwave Gourmet*

It felt as if every molecule in my body were in motion, as if only my skin were holding me together. I knew, rationally, what it was: sleep deprivation coupled with the tension I always felt when encountering Asia. I'd arrived in Hong Kong sometime during the night and had slept only a few hours, but I was too excited to stay in bed, so I dressed and went down to the coffee shop in the Mandarin Oriental for breakfast. That's when the rolling motions hit me, and I began seriously to wonder if I was going to hold it together.

The waiter handed me a menu, which I took with a visibly shaking hand. Neon-like, it flashed out at me: Oatmeal. Deliverance. It arrived in a steaming bowl on a plate with a paper lace doily, a silver pitcher of warm milk and a small bowl of raw sugar. My mother's voice reverberated in memory from a half-century away: There you go pumpkin, now you'll be just fine.

With every spoonful I became stronger; quiet settled into my center, I was my mother's brave girl, ready to face the teeming streets of Hong Kong. Saved again by the mystical bowl of oatmeal.

—Shirley Streshinsky

————

Molokai's famous Mule Ride hit the Kalaupapa trail again yesterday after a two-year layoff, and the poor mules got tired. They were out of shape. "They've been eating grass in the pasture," said mule skinner Buzzy Sproat. "It makes them fat but it doesn't give them zip. I'll feed them some high-octane oats."

—Bob Krauss, *Honolulu Advertiser*, Sept. 23, 1995

————

As a wee lad of eight, growing up in the small Irish town of Belleck, in the county Fermanagh, Ireland, I shared a fairly modest home with my family, including the aunt who raised me, a sister, a variety of dogs, a pony, and a beloved donkey named Rufus. I woke up one morning with a notion that I was not going to school that day and decided to convince my aunt that I was truly ill—not well enough for school mind you, but not sick enough to see the local pharmacist (the closest doctor was in the next county). Since my aunt was a firm believer that our daily oats (which I loved eating with Mother Kelly's Double Cream when we could afford it) were a cure-all, she decided to stir up a batch in the great black kettle that hung over the peat fire. She and I sat with our feet in front of the fireplace, warming our hands on the large steaming porcelain bowls of oatmeal. But after a few bites, Auntie thought something was missing. She opened the pantry door, and from behind the lovely Belleck china she retrieved a bottle of her favorite Irish whiskey, pouring a dram on her oatmeal and, winking at me, a bit less in mine. "Irish whiskey and oatmeal, that's the stuff," she proclaimed boldly as the aroma entered my nasal passages and I was filled with a warm glow. Mixed with brown sugar, warmed heavy cream, and that Irish amber fluid, my oatmeal had never tasted so good, and now I knew why Auntie believed so strongly in the curative power of oats.

—Seamus McManus is general manager of the Kahala Mandarin Oriental Hotel in Honolulu

—◦•◦—

In August of 1947, I was at the Salt Lake City airport for an early morning flight. I headed to the coffee shop for breakfast and slid onto a stool at the counter. A couple of stools away, reading the menu slowly and carefully, was a young cowboy. He said to the waitress: "I'd like to get some oatmeal, Ma'am."

The waitress said "sure," wrote it down and started to walk away.

"Ma'am," he called after her, "could I have that with brown sugar?"

"Sure," she made another note and started for the kitchen.

"And ma'am, could you put some raisins in it? Like maybe a handful, and a little pat of butter, with a sprinkle of cinnamon over it?"

She turned back to him. "And cream?"

He beamed. "That's right, but not that thin old Blue John milk, if you could get me a little pitcher full of real heavy cream I sure would appreciate it."

She studied him carefully, paused a moment, then she said: "You live with your mother, don't you?"

His face lit up. "How 'ju know?"

—Jon Brenneis is a photographer/raconteur. On the Salt Lake City trip where he met the Oatmeal Cowboy he was on assignment for Life Magazine. A few years later, finding himself in the early morning in yet another airport in another part of the country, he requested of the waitress: "Oatmeal, please, with a few raisins mixed in and some brown sugar sprinkled on top, if you will..." To which the waitress responded: "And I suppose you want a nickel in the bottom of the bowl?"

——◆——

According to the 28-ounce tin John McCann's Irish Oatmeal comes in, it is traditionally served with fresh buttermilk, but "Irish porridge is also good with milk or cream and brown sugar or honey, or with butter." Naturally.

——◆——

My dad was a high school athletic coach in Ripon, Wisconsin. All winter long he made breakfast in the morning for my two brothers and me. Oatmeal. Always. A great glob of it, and we were expected to eat every last bite. Dad believed that if you were going to play ball or run races or make good grades—as we were expected to do—you had to have a solid breakfast, and that was oatmeal. No two ways about it. I would sprinkle on some brown sugar, pour on the milk, and eat the top layer. Then, when Dad wasn't looking, I'd lower the bowl under the table and let our dog Mickey slurp down the rest. Mickey lived to a ripe old age.

—Babs Lester lives in Charlotte, North Carolina

Children age 12 and under eat an average of 48 bowls of oatmeal a year while adults age 65 and older average 68 bowls a year.

While mother was in the hospital giving birth to her eighth child, my dad—who was in the army—was in charge of making breakfast for the rest of us. It was oatmeal, cooked as best he could. My brother David took one look at the gray splat of oats in his bowl and made a sound of disgust. Retribution was swift and without mercy: Dad upended the bowl on David's head. The rest of us couldn't make our spoons fly fast enough to empty our bowls.

—B. J. Hughes lives and works in Honolulu

He always made oatmeal on Christmas morning, whether we wanted it or not.

—Anne Mitchell, as part of a loving remembrance of her father, Frederick Cleveland Mitchell, at his memorial service on February 11, 1996.

In the early 1980s, I took a series of meditation weekends called Enlightenment Intensives that helped me examine some deeper issues in my life.

I'm fairly skeptical of organized spirituality, but the Enlightenment Intensive technique of meditating, then talking with a partner, seemed to work. Once in a while I'd get a little flash of insight, in which the veil between me and ultimate reality would lift for a few seconds.

Halfway through the two-week Intensive in the winter of 1980, I discovered the real ingredient in oatmeal. I was at breakfast and feeling pretty zonked from five days of round-the-clock meditating. The weather was chilly, and the steaming oatmeal, laced with lines of melted butter, was especially comforting. As I gazed into my bowl, I suddenly saw the love in the oatmeal. Clear as day, I could see the love embodied by the warmth and the nourishment of this steaming, friendly porridge. And it wasn't that the oatmeal represented love; it was love. It was an overwhelming feeling that left me close to tears.

A few minutes later, I went over to the cook, a wonderful red-haired young woman named Namrata.

"I know what you've been putting in our food," I said in a fierce voice, pretending to scowl.

"What?" she asked, alarmed.

"The love."

"Oh, that. Of course."

—William Rodarmor is a French translator and the managing editor of *California Monthly*, the UC Berkeley alumni magazine.

By the fall of 1963, we were in Dublin, staying in a quiet, clean, separate-tables boarding house run by a woman known only as Maude. Here we were Irished up, learning all about Ireland and the Irish, and most of all, about Irish food and drink. In one corner of the sparsely furnished white dining room in the basement sat a range on which a pot of oatmeal appeared to be perpetually simmering. I had been a fan of oatmeal all my life, but now I was in Olympian oatmeal territory. Maude served it with a selection of additions: brown sugar, heavy cream, butter, currants, and black raisins. It was smooth, thick, and formidable. With it, she served the tea she served with everything else: Barry's Tea of Cork. After we had taken tea we understood why Mr. Barry had won the Empire Challenge Cup for Tea Blending. Barry's tea is still the biggest, boldest, roundest, toastiest, sunniest breakfast tea I have ever had. It warbled in perfect harmony with the oatmeal. It was like having breakfast across the table from Caruso and Melba singing love duets.

—Helen Gustafson in her book *The Agony of the Leaves—My Life in the Ecstasy of Tea*. Henry Holt and Company, Inc. © 1996

At my farm we use a lot of oats for feed, especially for the young horses and the old ones. Mostly as treats, and an important supplement to their diets. Oats are big socializers for the fillies and colts. These 500-pound babies are real terrors just after they are weaned from their mothers, and when you're around them you have to watch your back. They kick and snort and push each other around—they have absolutely no manners. They love oats, and they learn pretty quickly that when you are carrying around a bucket of oats you are a source of good things. Used as a treat, oats help the young horses learn to relate to people, so feeding becomes part of their training. "Sweet mix"—a prepared combination of oats, corn, and molasses—is fed to riding horses to help them keep weight on when they're working.

Oats make older horses happy and keep their coats shining. The kind of oats you give horses is pretty much like the rolled oats we make cookies with—easy for the old ones to chew and digest. Sumo, my big black horse who was once an Olympic jumper, doesn't need oats, but his best friend in the next stall does. So when Turtle gets his oats, Sumo has to have some too—or else his ears go back and he bangs his knees against the stall. All he needs is a handful of oats to make him happy and relatively quiet.

—Patricia Klaus, owner of Hawkwood Hill Farms

Alexander the Great fed his fabled horse, Esepheus, only oats. He claimed they made him run faster.

Race horse folks disagree on many things, including the best sign of the Zodiac by which to wean their foals, but they are unanimous in their agreement that heavy, clean oats are the best grain for race horses from start to finish. Thoroughbreds start a lifelong acquaintance with oats from eight to twelve weeks of age when oats are placed in creeps and the foals are allowed to eat as many as they want. From that time until the end of their days they will receive a grain ration composed of at least 50 percent oats.
   —W.P. Garrigus, University of Kentucky in the *Farm Quarterly*

Truly, a peck of provender: I could much your good dry oats. Methinks I have a great desire to a bottle of hay: good hay, sweet hay, hath no fellow.
   —Shakespeare, A Midsummer Nights Dream, IV, i 36

I eat oatmeal for breakfast.
I make it on the hot plate and put skimmed milk on it.
I eat it alone.
I am aware it is not good to eat oatmeal alone.
Its consistency is such that it is better for your mental health
if somebody eats it with you.
That is why I often think up an imaginary companion
to have breakfast with.
Possibly it is even worse to eat oatmeal with
an imaginary companion.
Nevertheless, yesterday morning, I ate my oatmeal—
porridge as he called it—with John Keats.

—Galway Kinnell, a selection from his poem "Oatmeal"

Rise and Shine

Classic Oat Scones

———

1 cup flour

1 cup rolled oats, quick or old-fashioned, finely ground in food processor

1 tablespoon sugar

2 teaspoons baking soda

1/4 teaspoon salt

1/4 cup butter

2 eggs

1/2 cup buttermilk

1/4 cup currants

Preheat oven to 350°. Mix dry ingredients well and cut in butter until fine. Beat together eggs, buttermilk, and currants. Make well in dry ingredients, pour in liquid, and mix quickly. To form scones, drop dough onto oiled baking sheet in two- to three-inch rounds. Bake for 15 to 20 minutes.

Makes 8 to 10 scones

Oatmeal Blueberry Scones

For several years now, after their early morning walks, Shirley and her friend Andrée have been stopping by Farah Jahansouz's Hopkins Street Bakery in Berkeley, California for coffee. Often they make up excuses to treat themselves to one of the amazing scones. (Be forewarned: they're addictive.)

2 cups all-purpose flour

1 3/4 cups cake flour

1/2 tablespoon baking powder

1 teaspoon soda

1/2 cup sugar

1 1/2 cups rolled oats, quick or old-fashioned

12 tablespoons salted butter

1/2 cup fresh or frozen blueberries

2 cups buttermilk

1 egg

Preheat oven to 375°. Mix dry ingredients, then add butter and blend by hand. Add blueberries and mix, then add buttermilk and stir just until it all comes together. Dough should be wet and sticky. On a lightly floured surface, shape dough into two balls. Gently wash with egg, sprinkle with cinnamon and sugar, and cut each ball into four portions. Bake for 20 to 25 minutes.

Makes 8 very large scones

Oat Bran Muffins

———◦———

2 1/2 cups uncooked oat bran

1 tablespoon baking powder

1/4 cup raisins or 1/4 mashed banana

1/2 teaspoon salt (optional)

3/4 cup milk or soy milk

2 eggs

1/2 cup maple syrup or honey

2 tablespoons oil

FILLING

Jam or Gorgonzola cheese (try jam for sweet
    muffins to serve at breakfast; use cheese for
    great savory muffins to serve with salads).

Preheat oven to 450°. Combine dry ingredients, mixing well. Beat liquids together, add to dry ingredients and stir until just moistened. Fill oiled muffin tins (or cupcake papers) one-third full, add the dollop of jam or cheese, then fill to two-thirds full. Bake 12 to 15 minutes or until done.

Makes 12 muffins

———◦———

The critical period in matrimony is breakfast-time.

—A.P. Herbert, Uncommon Law, p.98, 1935

Pecan-Oat Muffins

3/4 cup minced pecans

1 cup rolled oats, quick or old-fashioned

1/2 cup unbleached white flour

1/2 teaspoon baking soda

1 1/2 teaspoons baking powder

1/4 teaspoon salt (rounded measure)

1 cup buttermilk or yogurt

1 egg

4 tablespoons melted butter

6 tablespoons brown sugar

1/2 teaspoon vanilla extract

Preheat oven to 350° and lightly grease 12 muffin cups. Dry-roast the pecans and oats in a skillet over low heat for about 10 minutes, stirring frequently, until the oats are lightly browned.

Sift together flour, soda, baking powder, and salt into a medium-sized bowl. Stir in the toasted oats and pecans, and make a well in the center. In a separate container, beat together the remaining ingredients, and pour this mixture into the well. Mix just enough to blend. Fill the muffin cups 2/3 full, and bake for 15 to 20 minutes, or until a toothpick comes out clean.

Makes 12 muffins

From *The Enchanted Broccoli Forest* by Mollie Katzen (Ten Speed Press, 1995)

Breakfast Oat Muffins

From Sue Herodes, who claims to hate oatmeal, but loves these muffins.

1 16-ounce can pear slices
1 cup golden raisins
1/2 cup butter
3/4 cup honey
2 eggs
1 1/2 cups flour
1/2 cup uncooked oat bran
1 teaspoon baking powder
1/2 teaspoon baking soda
3 teaspoons cinnamon
3/4 teaspoon salt
1/8 teaspoon ground cloves
2 cups rolled oats

Preheat oven to 325°. Drain pears, reserving 1/2 cup syrup. Chop pears into small pieces. In a small saucepan, bring reserved syrup to a boil. Add raisins, remove from heat, and let stand 15 minutes. Cream butter, then beat in honey and eggs. Combine flour, oat bran, baking powder, baking soda, and seasonings and stir into butter mixture. Add raisins, syrup, and pears. Stir in oats. Pour 1/3 cup batter into oiled muffin tins. Bake for 20 minutes.

Makes 12 muffins

*"Eating oatmeal is sort of like kissing your sister...
not all that exciting."*

—Joe Munroe

Granola

5 cups rolled oats, quick or old-fashioned
1 cup chopped almonds
1 cup chopped cashews
1 cup powdered skim milk
1 cup soy flour
1 cup sesame seeds
1 cup sunflower seeds
1 cup honey
1 cup vegetable oil

Preheat oven to 300°. Mix all ingredients and spread out on 2 rimmed baking sheets. Cook for 30 minutes, or until lightly browned, stirring twice.

Makes about 10 cups

Muesli

This is a warm-weather favorite in Ritz-Carltons the world over.

4 cups rolled oats, quick or old-fashioned

1/2 cup coconut, toasted and dried

1/2 cup almonds, toasted

1/2 cup cranberries, dried

1 tsp. cinnamon powder

1 cup raisins

2 quarts half and half*

1 cup honey

1/2 cup granola (for garnish)

1 cup raspberries (or any seasonal, fresh fruit)

1 apple, shredded

Mix all dry ingredients. Whisk honey into the half and half until blended. Add to dry mix. Refrigerate overnight. Spoon into a serving bowl and sprinkle with granola, shredded apple, and fresh raspberries.

Serves 6 or more

---

*Executive chef Jean-Pierre Dubray of The Ritz-Carlton, San Francisco says that low- or nonfat milk can be used instead of half-and-half. All dry ingredients can be mixed ahead of time and stored in an airtight container.

Oatmeal Pancakes

The Junior League of Baton Rouge, Louisiana, came up with this pancake that die-hard Northern oat lovers swear by.

> 2 eggs
> 1/2 cup cottage cheese
> 1 tablespoon oil
> 1/4 cup rolled oats or 2 tablespoons rolled oats and
>   2 tablespoons wheat germ.
> 1/8 teaspoon salt

Place all ingredients in a blender or food processor and whir for 5 to 6 seconds, no more. Drop batter by tablespoons onto a hot, greased frying pan. Turn when pancakes bubble, and cook one minute more. Serve with jam, fruit preserves, or fresh berries.

Makes 6 to 8 pancakes

From *River Road Recipes II,* by the Junior League of Baton Rouge

Susan's Oatmeal Brûlée

The revenge of the oatmeal, from Susan Rosenblum Rabens.

This oatmeal brûlée was my answer to the agony of growing up in a large family—I was the oldest of eight—in Evanston, Illinois, where winters are cold, cold. Of course you had to have

something solid for your breakfast so you wouldn't freeze, something that would last you all day. The nature of oatmeal is to be lumpy and lie in your stomach like a lead ball. When my grandmother, who had grown up on a farm in Russia, came to live with us, she took over the ritual making of the oats. She was totally committed to the idea that every one of the eight of us would leave for school fortified with oatmeal. If any of us resisted, grandmother hadn't done her duty. Outright refusal was a personal affront to her integrity—she made sure you went off carrying a load of guilt. Luckily, breakfasts were so chaotic in our big family that now and then you could turn a bowl around without having put anything in it, but that didn't happen often. Mostly, we ate our oats.

I did promise myself that I would never serve lumpy oats to my own children—I make them with a whisk—and that someday, in retaliation, I would concoct a wonderful breakfast oat recipe.

> 1 cup rolled oats, quick or old-fashioned
> 1 3/4 cups water
> 1 apple, thinly sliced
> 4 tablespoons brown sugar
> cream or milk

Cook oats with water for about five minutes or until done. Pour cooked oatmeal (mixed with raisins, chopped prunes, or walnuts if you wish) into the bottom of individual ramekins or a shallow baking dish. Layer the top with apple slices. Sprinkle brown sugar over it all and put it under the broiler for a few minutes, until sugar melts and hardens. Add cream or milk.

Makes 2 large portions

Oatmeal Crème Brûlée

Jean-Pierre Dubray, executive chef at The Ritz-Carlton, San Francisco, offers this version of crème brûlée without the crème.

> 1 cup steel cut oats
> 6 cups water
>
> FRUIT COMPOTE (This can be done in advance)
> 1/2 cup sugar
> 1/2 cup water
> 2 cups of fresh seasonal berries such as diced straw-
>   berries, blueberries, blackberries, or raspberries.

To prepare oats, bring water to a boil, add the oats and simmer for 40 to 45 minutes, stirring occasionally. Adjust with water to desired consistency. For compote, bring water and sugar to boil; add berries and turn off heat.

Combine fruit compote with cooked oats, stirring gently together. Divide among 4 cereal bowls and coat top of each with 1 tablespoon of granulated sugar. Place under the broiler until the sugar is brown and caramelized.

Serves 4

Spare your breath to cool your porridge.

—*Rabelais, Works, bk V, 1552, ch 28*

Orange Oat Batter Bread

Perfect with morning coffee or afternoon tea.

> 3/4 cup milk
> 6 tablespoons sugar
> 1/2 teaspoon salt
> 5 tablespoons butter
> 1 teaspoon grated orange rind
> 1 tablespoon orange juice
> 1/4 cup very warm water
> 1 envelope active dry yeast
> 3 eggs, beaten
> 2 1/2 cups all-purpose flour
> 1/2 cup oat flour
> 1 cup dried currants

Heat milk, sugar, salt, and butter until butter is just melted. Cool to lukewarm. Stir in orange rind and juice and set aside. Measure water into a large bowl; sprinkle in yeast, and stir until dissolved. Add milk mixture and eggs. Blend in flours, 1 cup at a time. Beat until smooth. Stir in currants. Turn into greased 6-cup baking dish. Cover and let rise 45 minutes, or until doubled in bulk. Bake at 350° for 40 minutes, or until loaf is golden brown and gives a hollow sound when tapped. Cool a few minutes on wire rack, then remove bread from baking dish and cool.

Makes 1 loaf

Martha's Grandma's Oatmeal Bread

2 packages dry yeast
1/2 cup warm water
1 1/2 cups boiling water
1 cup rolled oats, quick or old-fashioned
1/2 cup molasses
1/3 cup shortening
1 tablespoon salt
5 1/2 to 6 cups flour
2 eggs, beaten

Soften yeast in warm water. In a separate large bowl, combine boiling water, oats, salt, molasses, and shortening. Cool to lukewarm. Stir in 2 cups flour, add eggs and beat well. Stir in yeast mixture. Beat well. Add rest of flour to make soft dough. Place dough in oiled bowl, cover, and refrigerate at least 2 hours or overnight. Turn onto floured board and shape into 2 loaves. Place in greased loaf pans. Cover. Let rise until doubled in size (about 2 hours). Bake 40 to 50 minutes at 375°.

Makes 2 loaves

Growing up in Idaho Falls meant "mush" for breakfast from October to April, and most of the time that was oatmeal. Even now when I eat oatmeal, I can close my eyes and see the pattern of the linoleum on our kitchen floor—tiny rust and red rectangles and squares, the yellow formica and chrome kitchen table and the box of Quaker Oats on the stove. Mother was a good Mormon. She had graduated from college in 1916—something usual for that time—but she really was an old-fashioned Victorian lady. She felt that her mission in life was to create a good home for her husband and children. She canned and baked and, in the winter, got up before anyone else to turn up the heat and set a formal breakfast table. By the time we came down, she would be dressed for the day, complete with an apron. Baking was her real forte; the kitchen always smelled wonderful. I can't remember her ever buying a birthday cake or a loaf of bread. Oatmeal was served with a little brown sugar melted on the top, some of the cream from the top of the milk bottle and, on occasion, her fabulous cinnamon rolls, if we were lucky.

Blizzards were part of winter in Idaho Falls. It could get down to ten or fifteen below zero, and the winds would howl. My sister and I walked to school, of course. Some mornings we would open the front door and it would be snowing so hard you couldn't see to the end of the walk. It didn't matter—we would pull on our snow suits and boots, wind a scarf around our faces until only our eyes were showing, and walk bravely into the storm—fortified and sustained by our mother's faith in hot mush for breakfast.

—Martha Vlahos

Methods

Oats were great for plugging up holes in a car's radiator.
Worked fine on my '37 Pontiac.

— Paul Wilson

GRUEL

gruel (grü-el) n., a light, usually thin, cooked cereal made by boiling meal, esp. oatmeal, in water or milk.

———

If she thought you looked poorly, my Grandma Brinker would cook up some gruel for "whatever's ailing you." She would toss "a little" oats into a bowl and cover them up with water. (I would be sent to the cistern to pump the water.) You'd let them stand "for as long as it took to milk a cow." You'd squeeze the water out of the oats and throw them to the chickens, while she commenced to simmer all the liquid on the woodstove "for a while." Sometimes she would add some honey, if the bees had been cooperative that year, or maybe a dusting of nutmeg or a teaspoonful of her fabulous strawberry jam. If the gruel was for Grandpa, she might add a splash of whatever was in the bottle on the top shelf.

—Shirley Streshinsky

STEEL CUT

The trick to preparing steel cut oats is to soak them overnight before cooking (at a ratio of one part oats to four of water); after that, you'll be addicted to their wonderfully nutty flavor. If you don't want to stand and stir, by all means defer to the microwave, which may have been invented with oatmeal in mind. Or if you have a Crock-pot, let the oats cook ever so slowly overnight.

IN THE MICROWAVE

The microwave revolutionized and revitalized the eating of oats. No more stirring, no more sticky pans left to soak in the sink—one dish does it all. The only annoying feature is the oats' habit of boiling over if you don't watch carefully, but that can be avoided by going to a lower power level and cooking several minutes longer.

THE OVERNIGHT OATMEAL METHOD

Place the top half of a double boiler directly on the stove. In it, bring three cups of water to a rapid boil, then gently and evenly pour one cup of rolled oats over the boiling water. Do not stir, but simmer for about five minutes. In the meantime, bring water to a boil in the bottom of the double boiler, place the oats on top, and turn off the heat altogether. Let it sit just like that overnight; next morning, simply turn on the heat under the double boiler. It should take 20 minutes or so to warm the oats, no stirring, no fuss.

Helen Gustafson grew up in St. Paul, Minnesota, where she began "a lifetime of oatmeal worship."

I have to limit my sugar, but my husband doesn't, so each morning, before I begin to cook our oats, I put two bowls in an oven warmed to about 200 degrees. One bowl is empty, and the other has a little water in it and some raisins. While our oats are cooking on the stove top, both bowls are warming and the raisins in his bowl are absorbing the water and plumping up. About two-thirds of the way through the cooking, I throw in about a third of a cup of oats, so the texture is part smooth and part chewy. At that point I also add a splash of low-fat milk—which ensures that wonderful but elusive white foam that sometimes bubbles up without the milk, and sometimes doesn't. I think brown sugar is much superior to white on oats, and a heavily flavored honey— that is to say, a wild honey—is even better.

My Aunt Bertha told me what to do with leftover oatmeal, but I have to say right off, this is tricky. You oil a loaf plan and press the oatmeal into it. Put it into the refrigerator, uncovered, for a day or two—until the oatmeal gets sufficiently dried out and solid enough to cut into slices that are thick enough to hold. If it is too moist, it will stick or break apart. There will probably be a crust on the top. Then you heat up a griddle, fry the slices in butter or a combination of butter and oil, and serve with tart red currant, raspberry, or wild plum jam, or even with chutney.

TOASTING OATS

Spread rolled oats (quick or old-fashioned) on a cookie sheet and toast them at 350° for 15 to 20 minutes.

VARIATIONS ON THE BASIC BOWL OF OATMEAL

There are probably as many ways to eat oatmeal as there are oatmeal eaters. There are those among the oatmeal literati who think how you eat your oats is a subtle indicator not only of character, but of your emotional stability. It is also true that we can learn something about the quality of parenting by observing how offspring are fed their oats—witness Bob Bones' childhood experience, below.

- Pat Landsberg takes her morning portion with vanilla yogurt, pecans, and dried cranberries.

- The chefs at The Ritz-Carlton, Boston cook up oats to order, stovetop, any way the customer wants them—sometimes heaped with a medley of fresh raspberries, blueberries, and strawberries and served, always, with a small silver pitcher of warm cream or milk.

- Judy Bianchi is a traditionalist: plain oats with a sliced banana, not overripe, on top, served with warm milk.

- Bob Bone liked oatmeal best when his mother drew pictures of Winnie the Pooh characters on top, so he could sing out when he gobbled up Eeyore and Pooh bear.

Ted Streshinsky's method is inviolate: one-half cup of thick cut rolled oats, left to soak for twenty minutes in three-fourths cup of cold water with one full tablespoon of orange marmalade stirred in. Then, cooked in the microwave for one and a half minutes at full power. No milk, no cream. Eaten, always, with a stainless steel tablespoon with a nice, round bowl.

———

On leisurely mornings, Shirley Streshinsky prefers to stand at the stove and stir steel cut oats (one cup oats to four of water) until the mystical white foam appears, and she feels in her bones (and her wrist) that the oats are perfect. Most of the time, she puts half a cup of thick cut oats in a nice big bowl with a cup of water and a few golden raisins, and cooks it in the microwave at level four for about five minutes. Then she sprinkles the top with whatever granola is on hand, pours on some one-percent milk, and knows that her day has been set in proper motion. If her cupboard is bereft of raisins and crunchy granola, she toasts raisin bread and spoons the oatmeal onto it, making a kind of open-faced sandwich.

———

Maria Streshinsky buys her oatmeal in the cafeteria at work—ready made.

In New York City, Mark Streshinsky and his wife Marie Plette use their friend Neal Harrelson's method:

1 1/2 cups water

1 tablespoon orange juice concentrate

1/2 apple, finely chopped

1/2 cup raisins or currants

1 banana, diced

2/3 cup rolled oats

1/3 cup oat bran

Boil water with fruit and juice concentrate. Add oatmeal and lower heat. Cook for about four minutes, stirring constantly. Add oat bran and continue to cook and stir one minute more.

David Streshinsky, his wife Sharon Kawamoto, and their son, Matthew, live in southern California and aren't that tuned into oatmeal...yet.

Scottish Oats: The Old-Fashioned Way

Oats. A grain, which in England is generally given to horses, but in Scotland supports the people.
 —Samuel Johnson, *Dictionary of the English Language*

A wily Scotsman's rejoinder: "Oh yes sire, in England they grow very fine horses, while in Scotland, we grow very fine people."

It was pleasant to me to find that "oats" the "food of horses" were so much used as the food of the people in Dr. Johnson's own town.
 —Boswell, *Life of Johnson*

I owe that by my definition of oats I meant to vex them (the Scots).
 —Samuel Johnson (1709-1785)

When I WAS little, my mother cooked my oatmeal with milk and sugar. Then, when I was about nine—when a Scots boy started to become a man—my dad took over and taught me how to eat it cooked with water with a little salt sprinkled on top. That was the traditional, old-fashioned way.

—Euan Findlay, Glasgow, Scotland

In 1327 the French chronicler Froissart noted that, on their journeys into England, Scottish soldiers never bothered with pots and pans, but seemed content to ride with a bag of oatmeal and a flat stone strapped between the saddle and the saddle cloth. When they got tired of a diet of stolen cattle they mixed up a paste of oatmeal and water and made little cakes, cooked on the stone among the campfire embers.

—*The Oat Cookbook*, Mary Cadogan and Shirley Bond

Scots are great walkers, and when they wander over the countryside they often take a pocketful of raw oats so they can enjoy a little "crowdie" (oats with fresh spring water) along the way. Porridge served hot in a Scottish kitchen comes with a bowl of cold milk alongside—for dipping into if a mouthful of oats proves too hot. Scots regularly serve up oats with ale or whiskey.

In Scotland, afternoon tea might include thin, hot oatcakes (pancakes), bannock buns (a quick bread), or clootie dumplings (a dense, fruit-cake-like pudding), all of this topped with something called Athol Brose—an ambrosia-like blend of oatmeal, butter, honey, cream, and whiskey.

Early in Scottish poet Robert Burns' career, he wrote "Address to a Haggis"— a haggis being a sort of mince or pudding made of sheep's entrails (liver, lungs, tongue, heart), onions, and oatmeal that had been toasted over an open fire, then stuffed together with some fat into the cleaned paunch of a sheep's stomach and boiled for hours. It is said to smell about as good as it sounds. The best things some folks could think to say about this concoction was that "it is said to be a good antidote to whiskey." Today's version of haggis features more lamb than innards, and is usually stuffed into sausage casings. (And, antidote to the contrary, on festive occasions such as New Year's, it is always offered with Scotch whiskey.) Clearly, haggis is an acquired taste; in Burns' ode, he made it abundantly clear that as far as he was concerned, real Scotsmen (mark the Rustic, haggis-fed) thrived on it.

Address To a Haggis

I

Fair fa' your honest, sonsie face,
Great chieftain o' the puddin-race!
Aboon them a' ye tak your place,
    Painch, tripe, or thairm:
Weel are ye wordy of a grace
        As lang's my arm

V

Is there that owre his French ragout,
Or olio that wad staw a sow,
Or fricassee wad mak her spew
    Wi' perfect sconner,
Looks down wi' sneering, scornfu' view
        On sic' a dinner?

VIII

Ye Pow'rs wha mak mankind your care,
And dish them out their bill o' fare,
Auld Scotland wants nae skinking ware
    That jaups in luggies;
But, if ye wish her gratefu' pray'r,
        Gie her a haggis!

Not Just for Breakfast

Oats: A cereal used essentially for the feeding of horses.

—*Le Petit Larousse, 1993 edition*

L'oat Cuisine: A Breton Galette

It is no understatement to say that the French are not partial to oats. But here, Anne Marie Humbert, a transplanted Bretonne, experiments with the galette, or crepe, that is a specialty of her part of France, adding a few oats to the buckwheat flour.

Anne Marie grew up in Brittany watching her grandmother make galettes on the tuile, a large cast iron skillet, over the fire in her big fireplace. "She would invite her friends for galette," Anne-Marie remembers fondly, "they would come, each bringing their own butter and eggs. In would go a pat of butter, then the egg... she made the *most wonderful* galettes." In Brittany, you can buy galettes in the stores, but none will have the texture that makes Anne Marie's unique—that comes from the oats.

CREPES

1 cup rolled oats
1 cup milk
2 tablespoons vegetable oil
2 eggs
1/4 cup buckwheat flour
1/4 cup white flour
2 tablespoons sugar
1 tablespoon baking powder
pinch of salt
3/4 cup water

FILLING

8 to 10 pats butter
8 to 10 slices ham
8 to 10 thin slices Gruyère or other swiss cheese
8 to 10 eggs, fried sunny side up
chopped shallots or parsley

Soak oats in milk for 5 minutes. Add oil and eggs and mix well. Sift together dry ingredients and mix quickly with wet ingredients until moist. Add water until batter is thin, as for crepes. Pour 1/4 cup batter onto sizzling hot griddle. Cook about 1 to 2 minutes on each side. To assemble: Place a pat of butter and one slice each of ham and cheese in the center of the galette, top with an egg, and garnish with a few chopped shallots or parsley. Fold crepes over to make a little package and voilà!

Makes 8–10 galettes

Zucchini Oat Frittata with Chicken-Apple Sausages

From Carol Kirk, who lives in Kensington, California.

> 4 eggs, beaten
> 1 tablespoon oil
> 1 tablespoon balsamic vinegar
> 1/2 teaspoon pepper
> dash Tabasco and Worcestershire
> 1/2 teaspoon hot sauce
> 1/4 cup oatmeal
> 1 bunch green onions, including some tops
> 2 cloves garlic
> 3 cups grated zucchini
> 1 cup grated sharp cheddar cheese
> 4 small (or 2 large) cooked chicken-apple sausages,
> sliced into small pieces

Preheat oven to 325°. Beat eggs. Stir in oil, vinegar, pepper, Tabasco, Worcestershire, and oatmeal. Add vegetables, cheese, and sausage and blend well. Pour into oiled 9 x 9 pan and bake 35 to 40 minutes, until center of frittata is firm.

Serves 8 as an appetizer or 4 as a main course

Walnut Oatmeal Burgers

1 1/2 to 3 cups walnut pieces

2 cups rolled oats

3 or 4 eggs, lightly beaten

1/2 cup skim milk

1 large onion, chopped fine

1 teaspoon sage

1 teaspoon salt

freshly ground black pepper

oil to brown patties

3 cups vegetable stock

Grind walnuts in blender and combine with oats, eggs, milk, onion, sage, salt, and pepper. Form patties to fit the size buns you'll be using. Brown patties on both sides in a lightly oiled skilled, then pour the stock into the skillet and bring to a boil. Reduce heat and simmer, covered, for 25 minutes. Serve on buns with "the fixins" or crumble and use as you would hamburger in chili, spaghetti sauce, etc.

Makes 8–12 burgers

Adapted from *Laurel's Kitchen*, by Laurel Robertson, Carol Flinders, and Brian Ruppenthal (Ten Speed Press, 1986)

Sesame-Oat Chicken or Fish

2/3 cup rolled oats, quick or old-fashioned, whirled
    in food processor until fine

1/3 cup olive oil

1 teaspoon thyme

1/2 teaspoon freshly ground pepper

1 tablespoon sesame seeds, toasted

1 1/2 pounds skinless, boneless chicken breasts or
    white fish fillets

lemon wedges

Toss oats with thyme, pepper, and sesame seeds. Dip chicken or fish in mixture until well coated. In heavy skillet, heat oil over moderately high heat. Fry until browned, about 4 minutes per side for chicken, 2 minutes for fish.

Serves 3

Sloppy Joes

Anyone who grew up eating oatmeal at home for breakfast probably remembers Sloppy Joes for lunch. Not exactly h'oat cuisine, but peculiarly, nostalgically satisfying on rainy, cold days...especially if you forego the sticky-sweet standard recipe for our version.

1 pound lean ground beef
1/2 cup chopped green pepper
1/2 cup chopped celery
1/2 cup chopped onion
1 cup water
1/2 cup rolled oats, quick or old-fashioned
1 teaspoon salt
1 cup tomato sauce mixed with 1/4 cup white
   vinegar and 2 tablespoons catsup

Brown beef with chopped vegetables; drain off any fat.

Add remaining ingredients, cook over low heat until thickened, and serve on English muffins or buns.

Makes 6–8 sandwiches

Naan Bread

Suna Kanga, who lives in Singapore but grew up in India, serves these with her Parsi curries.

3 1/2 cups white flour

1/2 cup oat bran

1 tablespoon sugar

1 tablespoon baking powder

1 1/3 teaspoons baking soda

1/2 tablespoon salt

2 eggs

1/4 cup yogurt

3/4 cup milk

6 teaspoons cooking oil

In deep bowl, combine dry ingredients and mix well. Make a well and add remaining ingredients. Mix until dough is sticky, adding a bit of warm water if needed.

Knead on floured board until dough is elastic. Pinch off golf ball size pieces and place on buttered pan. Cover with damp cloth for one hour. To bake, pat dough balls into thin circles about 6 inches in diameter. Put on sheet pan and bake in 450° oven until they puff up—about 2 1/2 minutes. Serve immediately.

Makes about 12 rounds

Bread with Steel Cut Oats

1 package dry yeast
2 cups warm milk
1/4 cup butter, melted and cooled
3 tablespoons. light brown sugar
1 cup steel cut oats
5 1/2 – 6 cups all-purpose flour
2 teaspoons salt
1 teaspoon ground ginger

Mix yeast, milk, butter, and brown sugar in large mixing bowl. Add oats, flour, salt, and ginger and mix until well blended. Knead dough about 10 minutes, until smooth and elastic. Pat into ball and put into oiled bowl, cover and let rise until doubled. Punch dough down, knead again, and shape into two round loaves. Place on floured baking sheets and let rise until doubled. With razor or sharp knife, cut circle around top of each loaf. Bake in middle of preheated 350° oven, about 40 minutes or until nicely browned and thumps* done.

Makes 2 loaves

*In bread making, one must master the art of thumping, i.e., plunking the bottom of the loaf until it gives the appropriate hollow "done" sound. Practice makes perfect.

Recipe adapted from *Monday Night at Narsai's—An international menu cookbook from the legendary restaurant,* by Narsai M. David and Doris Muscatine. ©1987 by Narsai M. David and Doris Muscatine.

Turkey Stuffing

Rolled oats make a exceptional substitution for stale bread. This recipe is offered by Sara Holtzapple, who puts it in the neck section of the turkey.

> *2 cups rolled oats, quick or old-fashioned*
> *1 1/2 teaspoons herbs (such as sage, rosemary, thyme, or other poultry seasoning)*
> *1 small onion, chopped*
> *1/2 cup butter, melted*

For a basic stuffing, mix oats with herbs and add onion and melted butter. Variations on the theme include the following additions:

> *celery, apples, and parsley*
> *apricot and lemon*
> *nuts and mushrooms*

Tim's Burst of Energy Bars

Tim Kuenster and Dave Silberman munched on these as they bicycled across America.

WHIRL IN FOOD PROCESSOR

1 cup uncooked oat bran

1/2 cup toasted sesame seeds

1/2 cup soy milk powder

2 tablespoons carob powder

1/2 cup cooked brown rice

MIX WELL WITH

1/2 cup raisins

*1/2 cup creamy peanut butter, at
   room temperature*

1/2 cup honey, at room temperature

Whirl oat bran, sesame seeds, soy milk and carob powders, and brown rice in a food processor. Mix well with raisins, peanut butter, and honey. There's no need to bake—just spread the mixture on an oiled pan until about 1/4 inch thick and refrigerate it overnight. Cut into rectangular pieces.

Trail Mix

Before heading off on a long hike, go to the bulk food department of your favorite health food store or grocery store and pick a variety of your favorite things. Balance out sugar-heavy items to protein- and carbohydrate-heavy items. Stay away from small items because they fall to the bottom of the bag, and you end up with flaky, hard to grasp stuff.

WINTER VERSION (FOR COLD, CRISP DAYS)

On cold, crisp days, try the following (just throw handfuls together in a plastic bag):

> *Your favorite granola*
>
> *Yogurt-covered peanuts (peanuts are a good source of protein, iron, and niacin, and the toppings make them taste good!)*
>
> *Almonds (rich in protein, iron, calcium, and vitamin B2)*
>
> *Cashews*
>
> *Dried cranberries or raisins or both (natural sugar, good source of quick energy)*
>
> *Thick cut rolled oats (good source of fiber)*
>
> *M&Ms (one more kick of sugar to get you up the last steep hill)*
>
> *Shredded coconut (for decoration)*

Replace covered peanuts and M&Ms (anything that melts) with minioatmeal-currant cookies, which you can get at most health food stores.

Oatmeal has traveled to the North Pole, the South Pole, and Mt. Everest with expeditioners and has orbited the earth with U.S. astronauts.

In 1932, Americans in small towns across the country celebrated the bicentennial of George Washington's birth with lectures, tea parties, tree plantings, and many colonial balls. In Cedar Rapids, Iowa, painter Grant Wood ("American Gothic") was on the organizing committee of the Beaux Arts Ball, where celebrants were to come "in the colonial garb of George Washington's administration." Wood, who loved costume parties, won a prize for his ensemble: the man on the Quaker Oats box.

® the Quaker Oats Company

Just Desserts

Your Classic Oatmeal Cookie

———

1 cup brown sugar
1 cup white sugar
1 cup butter
2 eggs
2 teaspoons vanilla
2 cups flour
1 teaspoon baking powder
1/2 teaspoon salt
2 1/2 cups rolled oats, quick or old-fashioned
1 cup raisins

Preheat oven to 350°. Cream sugars and butter together. Beat in eggs and vanilla. Sift together flour, baking powder, and salt and add to butter mixture. Stir in oats and raisins and blend well. Drop large tablespoonfuls onto an oiled cookie sheet and bake for 10 to 15 minutes.

Makes about 4 dozen cookies

Sasha's Oatmeal Delights

Karen Dash says, "While I'm waiting for my children to come of age, oatmeal-wise, I am comforted knowing they are getting some of oatmeal's benefits when they devour these cookies, named for my daughter."

1 cup butter or margarine

1 cup brown sugar, firmly packed

1 cup granulated sugar

2 eggs

1 teaspoon vanilla

1 1/2 cups flour

1 teaspoon salt

1 teaspoon baking soda

3 cups rolled oats, quick or old-fashioned

1 cup chocolate chips

1/2 cup chopped walnuts

1/2 cup coconut, flaked and sweetened

Cream butter and sugars. Add eggs and vanilla. Beat well. Sift together flour, salt, and soda; add to butter mixture. Stir in oats, chocolate chips, nuts, and coconut. Mix. Form dough into rolls, wrap in plastic wrap and chill 1 hour. When dough is chilled, pre-heat oven to 350°. Slice dough 1/2-inch thick and place rounds on a baking sheet. Bake 10 minutes.

Makes about 5 dozen cookies

Oatmeal Fudge Squares

Anne Stewart says this not only gives quick energy, but survives backpack transport on the ski slopes.

1 cup butter (2 sticks)

2 cups brown sugar

2 eggs

2 teaspoons vanilla

2 1/2 cups flour

1 teaspoon baking soda

1 teaspoon salt

3 cups rolled oats, quick or old-fashioned

1 cup nuts

FUDGE LAYER

1 14-ounce can condensed milk

1 12-ounce package semi-sweet chocolate chips

2 tablespoons butter

1/2 teaspoon salt

1 teaspoon vanilla

1 1/2 cups chopped nuts

Preheat oven to 350°. Cream butter and sugar. Add vanilla and eggs and stir well. Mix flour, baking soda, and salt and gradually add to butter mixture. Slowly add oats and nuts and blend well.

For fudge layer, melt chocolate in condensed milk in a double boiler. Remove from heat and add remaining ingredients. Stir until butter is melted.

To assemble, pat 2/3 of the oat mixture into the bottom of a 10 x 15-inch pan, compacting well with fork tines. Spread chocolate mixture over the top. With fingers, crumble the rest of the oat mixture evenly over the chocolate so that the chocolate is covered. Bake for 25 minutes. Cool and cut into squares.

Oatmeal-Chocolate Chip Drops

Susan Rabens is an expert baker who lives in Berkeley but grew up in Evanston, Illinois.

> *1 cup butter*
> *2 egg yolks*
> *1 cup powdered sugar*
> *2 cups flour*
> *1/2 cup rolled oats, quick or old-fashioned*
> *1 1/3 cups semisweet chocolate chips*

Preheat oven to 325°. Beat yolks and butter together. Add sugar and flour. Stir in oats and chocolate chips. Drop by teaspoonfuls on baking sheet and bake 10-15 minutes. After cookies have cooled, sprinkle with more powdered sugar.

Makes about 40 cookies

Bob's Oatmeal Raisin Cookies

Bob Gerner's cookies are definitely a contender for the semi-classic title.

> 1/2 cup butter
>
> 1 cup raw (turbinado) sugar
>
> 1 egg
>
> 1 teaspoon vanilla
>
> 3/4 cup whole wheat pastry flour
>
> 1/2 teaspoon baking soda
>
> 1 1/2 cups rolled oats, quick or old-fashioned
>
> 1/2 cup raisins
>
> 1/2 cup chopped walnuts

Preheat oven to 350°. Cream butter, adding sugar gradually. Add egg and vanilla and mix well. Sift flour once with soda, and add oatmeal, raisins, and walnuts. Combine thoroughly with butter and sugar mixture. Drop by tablespoonfuls on an oiled cookie sheet and bake for 10 to 15 minutes.

Makes 2 1/2 dozen.

Until the age of one and a half, I have been told, I had a voracious appetite. Then I got a roaring case of the chicken pox which lasted for three months. After that, I had no appetite for food at all.

For years, my diet was toast and hot cereal—wheat hearts, cream of wheat, and oatmeal. About eighty percent of the time, oatmeal. I had it for breakfast, lunch, and dinner. My mother and father—who was a butcher—tried everything. Even, just once, a spanking, to which I responded by refusing to eat anything. Finally my uncle, who was a doctor, told them to leave me to my oatmeal, and they did. We had something called HO Oats, a thick rolled oat. I took it with a pat of butter and some brown sugar. Our family would sit down to Sunday dinner, maybe it would be a roast with potatoes and green peas. I'd head to the kitchen for some oats. My main memories of growing up were about food. I had my first hot dog at about age five, my first hamburger when I was in the sixth grade. Gradually, I added other foods. By the time I got out of high school I was eating plain mashed potatoes. No gravy.

My second year in college, all I could afford to eat was oatmeal and brown rice. Somehow my roommate and I managed to get some cases of canned peaches, and we lived on that all year. About once a week we'd add some hamburger and green onions. That entire year, all I thought about was food.

After that, I worked in the college restaurant, so I had a key to the kitchen. At night I'd go there and make granola, which I would then sell to the students. Since then I've always worked with food. Now I buy 40,000 pounds of oats at a time for my health food business.

—Bob Gerner is the owner of natural foods stores in San Francisco's East Bay

Cranberry Crisp

The British call them "crumbles," the Americans say "crisps"—either way, oats are perfect.

> 2 cups cranberries
> 2 cups chopped, peeled apples
> 1 cup raisins
>
> TOPPING
> 1 cup sugar
> 1 1/2 cups rolled oats, quick or old-fashioned
> 1 cup brown sugar
> 1/2 cup butter

Preheat oven to 350° and butter an 8-inch square baking dish. Combine cranberries, apples, and raisins, and spread in baking dish. Crumble remaining ingredients together and spread over fruit. Bake 1 hour and serve warm with whipped cream.

Serves 6 to 8

Ginger Apple Crisp with Yogurt

A good old down-home country favorite, with a ginger kiss.

6 cups sliced apples
1 tablespoon thinly sliced fresh ginger
1 tablespoon lemon juice

TOPPING
1/2 cup sugar
1 teaspoon cinnamon
1/4 teaspoon salt
1/2 cup butter
3/4 cup rolled oats, quick or old-fashioned

Preheat oven to 350° and butter an 8-inch square baking dish. Toss apples with ginger and lemon juice and spread in baking dish. In a separate bowl, sift together sugar, cinnamon, and salt, and cut in butter until coarse. Stir in oats and sprinkle mixture over the apples. Bake 50 to 60 minutes and serve warm with fresh plain yogurt.

Serves 6 to 8

Almond-Oatmeal Apple Crisp

6 tart apples, peeled and sliced

1 cup sugar

1/2 teaspoon cinnamon

2 teaspoons lemon juice

TOPPING

6 tablespoons butter

3/4 cup rolled oats, quick or old-fashioned, whirled
    for a few minutes in a food processor or blender

1/2 cup sliced almonds

Preheat oven to 350° and butter an 8-inch square baking dish. Toss apples with half the sugar and the cinnamon and lemon juice. Spread in baking dish. Cut the remaining sugar, butter, and oats into a crumbly mixture. Mix in nuts. Sprinkle evenly over the apples. Bake 45 minutes to 1 hour and serve warm with fresh plain yogurt.

Serves 6 to 8

*"Oh no," cried Baby Bear, in his tiny little voice.
"Someone's been eating my porridge, and they've eaten it all up!"*

—Baby Bear, in "Goldilocks and the Three Bears"

---

*Sowing wild oats. To engage in youthful indiscretions,
usually sexual liaisons: "Paul asked his father if
he had sowed his wild oats before getting married."*

—Dictionary of Cultural Literacy

When I was growing up, no sugared dry breakfast cereal was
allowed in our house, ever. No Lucky Charms, No Froot Loops, no
Cocoa Puffs. An exception was made once a year for our family
vacation at the beach. Then we were allowed Honey Nut Cheerios.
It took us a while to realize that Cheerios were in the shape of an
"o" for a reasons: the principal ingredient is oats.

—Maria Streshinsky

Apple Pan Dowdy

Not exactly old-fashioned, and forget the shoo-fly pie.

> 1/4 cup steel cut oats
> 3/4 cup water
> 4 cups apples, pared and sliced (Gravensteins
>   are good)
> 3/4 cup sugar
> 1 teaspoon cinnamon
>
> PASTRY
> 3/4 cup + 2 tablespoons flour
> 2 tablespoons oat bran
> 1/2 cup butter
> 1/2 teaspoon salt
> 2 tablespoons cold milk

Preheat oven to 300° and butter an 8-inch square baking dish. Mix oats and water and cook for two minutes in the microwave. Combine oats with apples, sugar, and cinnamon and spread in baking dish.

To make pastry, mix salt into flour and cut in butter until crumbly. Quickly add water, blend, and gather into a ball. Roll out on floured pastry board to size of baking dish. Place pastry on top of fruit mixture and cut steam openings. Bake 1 hour and 15 minutes. Serve with yogurt or ice cream.

Serves 4

"The Best Brownie in the World"

...says Susan Kepner, who translates Thai books when she isn't making brownies.

1/2 cup butter

3 ounces (3 squares) semisweet chocolate

2 eggs

1 cup sugar

1 teaspoon vanilla

2/3 cup oat flour

1/2 cup nuts (optional)

FROSTING

1 ounce (1 square) semisweet chocolate

1 cup confectioners sugar

1 tablespoon butter

1/2 teaspoon vanilla

1 teaspoon milk

Preheat oven to 350°. Melt butter and chocolate over low heat, stirring constantly. Cream eggs and sugar together and add to chocolate. Stir in vanilla, then add flour and nuts and mix well. Spread in 8 x 8-inch pan and bake for 25 minutes. For frosting, melt chocolate and butter in top of double boiler, stir in vanilla and sugar, and add enough milk to bring to spreading consistency.

Makes 16 brownies

Marjorie's Savannah Splash Peach Pie

For Marjorie Stafford, the "splash" is bourbon. Marjorie, an artist and decorator, grew up in St. Louis, Missouri and now lives in Fort Lauderdale.

PIE CRUST

3/4 cup all purpose flour and 1/2 cup oat flour

1 teaspoon sugar (optional)

1/2 teaspoon salt

1/4 cup butter, chilled

3 tablespoons vegetable shortening, chilled

2 1/2-3 tablespoons cold water

FILLING

2 1/2 pounds or 6 cups pared fresh peaches, sliced evenly into mixing bowl

2 teaspoons lemon juice or a splash of bourbon

1/2 cup light brown sugar

3 tablespoons flour

1/4 teaspoon salt

1/4 teaspoon cinnamon

1/2 cup firmly packed light brown sugar

4 tablespoons softened butter

3 tablespoons all purpose flour

3 tablespoons rolled oats, quick or old-fashioned

1/4 teaspoon salt

1/2 teaspoon fresh grated nutmeg

1 teaspoon cinnamon

1/2 cup chopped pecans

Preheat oven to 400°. To prepare pie crust, combine all ingredients, adding cold water last. Mix quickly with pastry cutter. On a floured board, roll dough to 1/4" thickness. Fit dough into a 9-inch pie pan.

For the filling, mix flour, salt, and cinnamon. Toss mixture quickly with peaches, lemon juice or bourbon, and brown sugar and turn into pastry-lined pie pan.

Mix streusel topping ingredients together with a fork until crumbly. Sprinkle over top of pie. Bake 30 to 40 minutes, lowering heat to 375° after 15 minutes.

Makes 1 pie

Roberto's Biscotti all'Avena

Roberto Soncin Gerometta is a photographer who grew up in Venice, Italy.

3 1/2 cups unbleached flour
1 cup semolina flour
1 cup uncooked oat bran
1 teaspoon baking powder
pinch of salt
1 cup sugar
1 cup butter, chilled
3 large eggs
parchment paper for lining pans

Preheat oven to 350°. In a large bowl, mix together flours, oat bran, baking powder, and salt. Blend well. Add sugar and mix. Cut in butter until fine. Make well in center and drop in eggs. Work with hands until blended. Roll out until very thin, about 1/8 inch. Cut into 2-inch squares and bake on parchment paper-lined pans for about 20 minutes, until golden brown.

Makes 16 biscotti

When I was a little boy of seven years of age, I spent the summer holidays in a retreat that was managed by the nuns Imeldine, the same nuns who taught at the grammar school I was attending in Venice. My father was well aware that the nuns could not be as generous with us as he would have liked, so he sent us off with an assortment of food supplies. The items that I remember the most were these large cartons filled with little packages of "Biscotti all'Avena Lazzaroni" made by one of the best names of Italian food. Squarish, flat, golden brown, semi-sweet, very fragrant, the mystery of youth and memory. We would slip one little package of biscotti in our knapsacks and once we finished the food given us by the nuns, as we were walking in the meadows of the Dolomiti mountains around the village of Sappada, we would break open the wrapping, inhale the sweet scent of the biscotti, bite into one and go to heaven, compliments of my father.

—Roberto Soncin Gerrometta

ANZAC Biscuits

In Australia and New Zealand, April 25 is ANZAC Day (for Australia New Zealand Army Corps)—a solemn celebration of military defeat and an appalling loss of life by the army of the newly created Commonwealth of Australia in its initial engagement in the First World War. At dawn on that fateful April day, the Anzacs arrived in the Dardanelles, intent on helping the British wrest the Gallipoli peninsula from the Turks. In the days and months that followed, 33,532 soldiers died, among them 8,587 Australians, before the British admitted defeat and withdrew.

On the homefront, the women did what they could, and baked biscuits (aka cookies) forever after called "Anzac biscuits." The Anzac troops received them in food parcels from home. With eggs in short supply, the homefronters made do—the truly authentic recipes call for "Lyle's Golden Syrup."

1 cup flour

1 cup sugar

1/4 teaspoon salt

1 cup flaked coconut

1 cup rolled oats, quick or old-fashioned

1 teaspoon baking soda

2 tablespoons boiling water

3 tablespoons golden syrup

1/2 cup butter, melted

Preheat oven to 350°. Mix flour, sugar, salt, coconut, and rolled oats together. In another bowl, dissolve baking soda in the boiling water. Stir in golden syrup and melted butter. Mix all ingredients together and place by teaspoonfuls on a well-oiled or nonstick oven tray. Bake for approximately 15 minutes until golden brown. Cool and store in airtight container.

Makes about 2 dozen cookies

Oatmeal-Almond Wafers

3 eggs, beaten

2 cups sugar

2 tablespoons butter

3/4 teaspoon vanilla (or 1/2 teaspoon almond extract)

1 teaspoon salt

1 cup sliced almonds

2 cups rolled oats. quick or old-fashioned

Preheat oven to 350°. Mix sugar and eggs very gradually, beating all the while. Melt butter and add to sugar mixture. Add vanilla and salt. Gently stir in almonds and rolled oats. Drop onto baking sheet by the teaspoonful about an inch apart and bake for 10 minutes, until wafers are pale brown and shiny on the bottoms. (Save yourself some major grief by lining pans with parchment paper; then all you do is let them cool a bit and peel them off.)

Makes 3 to 4 dozen

An Old-Fashioned Oatmeal Cake

Carol Kirk takes this cake to their mountain cabin every summer to feed a gang.

CAKE
1 cup rolled oats
1 1/4 cups boiling water
1/2 cup shortening
1 cup brown sugar
1 cup white sugar
2 eggs
1 teaspoon vanilla
1 1/2 cup sifted flour
1/2 teaspoon salt
1/2 teaspoon cinnamon
1 teaspoon soda

TOPPING (the best part)
6 tablespoons butter
1 cup nut meats
1 cup coconut
1/2 cup cream
1 teaspoon vanilla
2/3 cup brown sugar

Preheat oven to 350°. Mix oats, boiling water, and shortening and let cool. Add sugars, eggs, and vanilla. Mix flour, salt, cinnamon, and soda and add to mixture. Spread in 10 x 14-inch pan and bake for 30-35 minutes. Let cake cool and prepare topping. Stir topping ingredients together over low heat until blended. After cake has cooled, spread topping and place under the broiler for one minute.

Serves 12

*On hot summer days at the end of the 19th century,
millers spiked their workers' barrels of drinking water with oat flour,
believing it would give them energy.*

—*Brands, Trademarks and Good Will, by Arthur Marquette*

Bibliography

B., Philip. *Blended Beauty*. Berkeley, CA: Ten Speed Press, 1995

Cambridge Encyclopedia. New York: Cambridge University Press, 1994

Columbia Encyclopedia, 5th edition. New York: Columbia University Press, 1993

Cadogan, Mary and Shirley Bond. *The Oat Cookbook*. London: Macdonald & Co. Publishers Ltd., 1987

David, Narsai and Doris Muscatine. *Monday Night at Narsai's*. New York: Simon & Schuster, 1987

Gustafson, Helen. *The Agony of the Leaves: My Life in the Ecstasy of Tea*. New York: Henry Holt & Co., 1996

Junior League of Baton Rouge, Louisiana. River Road Recipes II. (800) 204-1726

Katzen, Mollie. *The Enchanted Broccoli Forest*. Berkeley, CA: Ten Speed Press, 1995

Kinnell, Galway. *When One Has Lived a Long Time Alone*. New York: Alfred A. Knopf, Inc., 1990

Marquette, Arthur. *Brands, Trademarks and Good Will: The Story of the Quaker Oats Company*. New York: McGraw Hill, 1967

Robertson, Laurel and Carol Flinders and Brian Ruppenthal. *The New Laurel's Kitchen*. Berkeley, CA: Ten Speed Press, 1986